French Festivals and Traditions

Activities and Teaching Ideas for KS3

Nicolette Hannam and Michelle Williams

Brilliant
PUBLICATIONS

Dedication
In memory of my lovely mum, Pauline Cranfield.
Michelle Williams.

We hope you and your pupils enjoy learning about the festivals and traditions in this book. Brilliant Publications publishes many other books for teaching modern foreign languages. To find out more details on any of the titles listed below, please log onto our website: **www.brilliantpublications.co.uk**.

Published by Brilliant Publications
Unit 10
Sparrow Hall Farm
Edlesborough
Dunstable
Bedfordshire
LU6 2ES, UK

E-mail: info@brilliantpublications.co.uk
Website: www.brilliantpublications.co.uk

General information enquiries:
Tel: 01525 222292

The name Brilliant Publications and the logo are registered trademarks.

Written by Nicolette Hannam and Michelle Williams
Illustrated by Sarah Wimperis
Front cover designed by Brilliant Publications

Contents

Month	Mois	Festival/Tradition

Introduction

French Festivals and Traditions was written by two teachers to provide information about festivals and traditions in France in response to the revised *KS3 Framework for Modern Foreign Languages*:

'Contexts for learning should give pupils opportunities to explore aspects of the life and culture of countries and communities where the language is spoken. These could include people, places, festivals, national events, food, sport, history, education, climate, geographical features, buildings, the spoken and the written word, music and song, the visual arts and the media.' (*KS3 Framework Modern Foreign Languages*).

Addressing Intercultural Understanding (strand 3), and the importance of 'appreciating cultural diversity', this book introduces cultural aspects of everyday life in other countries via a month-by-month account. Every month has a variety of ideas, suggested teaching ideas, vocabulary and photocopiable guided sheets.

French Festivals and Traditions also provides opportunities to exploit ever important cross-curricular links in support of CLIL.

Analysis grids show how the ideas in this book can be linked with the learning objectives of the *KS3 Framework for Modern Foreign Languages*, making it an invaluable tool for lesson planning and preparation.

French Festivals and Traditions KS3
© Nicolette Hannam, Michelle Williams and Brilliant Publications

Analysis by year group

How this book links to the Framework. Examples by year group and strand.

Year Group		Learning Objectives
7	**Strand 1**	**Listening and Speaking**
	1.1	Identify gist and some detail in face to face exchanges, spoken passages, stories and songs
	1.4	Make effective use of simple verbal or visual prompts
	1.5	Plan and present a short talk or narrative, speaking clearly, audibly and with accurate pronunciation
Examples		Les contes de fées (pages 27–31) Comparing pastimes and everyday life (pages 56–57) Cuisine française (page 65–69) Christmas carols (page 73)
	Strand 2	**Reading and Writing**
	2.1	Identify main points and some detail in written passages, stories and poems
	2.3	Select a text for personal reading
	2.4	Use sentences and paragraphs as models for their own writing
	2.5	Make effective use of familiar language in different text types
Examples		Les contes de fées (pages 27–31) Recipes (pages 11, 14, 60) Menu (page 53) Cards (pages 16, 24, 34, 37)
	Strand 3	**Intercultural Understanding**
	3.1	Appreciating cultural diversity Investigate an aspect of life and compare with their own, noting similarities and differences
	3.2	Recognizing different ways of seeing the world Explore interests and opinions of young people, and compare with their own Reflect on and challenge stereotypes
Examples		Comparing pastimes (page 57) Role models (page 64) La rentrée (pages 51–55) How are cultures of different countries incorporated ... (pages 49 –50)

Analysis by year group

Year Group	Learning Objectives	
8	**Strand 1**	**Listening and Speaking**
Examples	1.3	Identify and use specific language for a range of communicative functions Les contes de fées (pages 27–31) Poisson d'avril (pages 22–23) Games vocabulary (page 25) Christmas carols (page 73)
	Strand 2	**Reading and Writing**
Examples	2.1	Develop their vocabulary through contact with authentic materials
	2.4	Use a story, poem or information text as a stimulus for their own writing Les contes de fées (pages 27–31) Recipes (pages 11, 14, 60) Menu (page 53) Cards (pages 16, 24, 34, 37)
	Strand 3	**Intercultural Understanding**
Examples	3.1	Identify and explain an aspect of life that has changed over time
	3.2	Investigate aspirations of young people, recognizing perspectives that are both similar to and different from their own Mardi gras (page 19–21) La fête du travail (pages 32–33) Le quatorze juillet (pages 41–44) Self portrait (page 57) Role models (page 64)

French Festivals and Traditions KS3
© Nicolette Hannam, Michelle Williams and Brilliant Publications

Analysis by year group

Year Group		Learning Objectives
9	**Strand 1**	**Listening and Speaking**
Examples	1.1	Understand longer sequences of speech, noting relevant points for oral feedback and discussion Les contes de fées (pages 27–31) Adapt information about Cannes film festival (page 39) and Beaujolais nouveau (page 70)
	Strand 2	**Reading and Writing**
Examples	2.1	Identify and summarize evidence from a text
	2.4	Adapt a text for a different audience and purpose Les contes de fées (pages 27–31) Christmas Carol (page 73) Recipes (pages 11, 14, 60) Games vocabulary (page 25) Pupils can choose one idea or topic and develop a PowerPoint presentation aimed at a given audience
	Strand 3	**Intercultural Understanding**
Examples	3.1	Develop and communicate an in-depth understanding of an aspect of culture that they have identified and researched
	3.2	Understand how attitudes towards other countries and reactions to world events may differ from those of their own culture La fête des Rois (pages 9–12) Mardi gras (page 19–21)

Successful teaching Ideas for new vocabulary

There are many ways to help pupils learn new vocabulary and it is important to use a variety of methods and make it fun. Below are some successful ideas that have been tried and tested:

◆ Very simply, hold up flashcards and ask the pupils to repeat the words after you. They like doing this in different voices.

◆ Mime a card. Pupils have to guess the word, in French.

◆ Which flashcard am I holding? Hold the flashcard facing you. Ask pupils to guess which one you are looking at. This tests memory and pronunciation.

◆ True or False. Pupils only repeat the flashcard after you if you are saying the word that matches it.

◆ Matching cards. Give out cards to match yours, for example with names of pets. Say a word and pupils hold up the matching card, if they have it.

◆ Pupils could sequence the words as you call them out.

◆ Pupils could stand in order with flashcards, for example, with names of the months. Or they could stand in alphabetical order.

◆ For colours, they could build towers in the order that you call out, using coloured bricks.

◆ Pupils could hold up key words as they hear them in a song.

◆ Pupils could draw what you say, using mini-whiteboards.

◆ Slap the flashcard! Or the correct part of a picture (for example, the face). Pupils come up to the board in pairs (boys versus girls is popular). They use their hands to touch (slap) the flashcard the teacher says. A point is given to the first one to touch the correct flashcard.

◆ Teach the pupils actions to go with the songs you learn.

◆ Use puppets or soft toys to ask and answer questions.

◆ Give the pupils cards with words and pictures and use them to play Pelmanism (also known as Pairs).

◆ As above, but play Snap.

◆ Picture lotto. Cross off pictures as you hear the word called out.

◆ Pictionary. The teacher can draw pictures, for example pets, and pupils call out as soon as they recognize it. Or they can play in small groups, on mini-whiteboards.

◆ Hangman /Le pendu.

◆ Jacques dit.

◆ Chinese Whispers.

◆ Kim's Game.

French Festivals and Traditions KS3
© Nicolette Hannam, Michelle Williams and Brilliant Publications

Le Jour de l'An/ La fête des Rois

New Year's Day/ Epiphany

Background information

French people usually spend *Le Jour de l'An* (New Year's Day) '*en famille*', celebrating with their family, wishing each other '*bonne année*' (Happy New Year).

La fête des Rois (Epiphany or King's/Queen's Festival) takes place on the first Sunday in January. It is often celebrated with family. *Une galette* is a round cake which has a small object hidden inside, called *une fève*. It is served with a paper crown on the top. *Une fève* means 'a broad bean' and traditionally dried beans were used. Nowadays *la fève* is usually a ceramic charm placed discreetly in the galette. The person who finds *la fève* has won and has to wear the crown, becoming King or Queen.

Usually the youngest person in the family, hides under the table and says who is going to have which piece of the cake, so there is no cheating! The cake is divided into enough pieces for everyone, plus one extra called 'la part du pauvre'.

One of the origins of *la galette des Rois* dates back to the 11th Century when monks elected their future leader by placing a silver coin in a loaf of bread. This custom then spread to other monasteries.

La fête des Rois commemorates Twelfth Night when the Three Kings arrived in Bethlehem bearing gifts for baby Jesus. In the 1960s ceramic figures started to replace the traditional dried bean, encouraging you to buy and collect more charms. Today, you can collect sets of charms, even Disney-themed ones.

You can buy *galettes* in every *boulangerie* (bakery) throughout the month of January.

The *galette* should be served warm, with a very dry white wine or champagne (for adults only!).

Teaching ideas

◆ Explain to the pupils about the tradition of *La fête des Rois*.

◆ Pupils mime making a *galette* as you give instructions in French (see recipe on page 11).

◆ Make the *galette* (see page 11) and celebrate *La fête des Rois* in class. Use a soft bean or sweet as *la fève*.

◆ Role play buying a *galette* in a *boulangerie*.

◆ Discuss and compare how New Year is celebrated here and in France.

◆ Make *bonne année* cards to take home. Include details of what pupils will learn in the next two terms, to inform parents. Note: when writing *bonne année* on cards you use capital letters (*Bonne Année*), but normally it isn't capitalized.

Vocabulaire

bonne année	Happy New Year
une galette	a special cake
une fève	a broad bean/ charm
un roi	a king
une reine	a queen
une boulangerie	a bakery
une couronne	a crown
en famille	as a family
la pâte feuilletée	puff pastry
la pâte d'amande	marzipan
un œuf	an egg

French Festivals and Traditions KS3
© Nicolette Hannam, Michelle Williams and Brilliant Publications

La galette des Rois

Ingredients
500 g puff pastry
1 dry bean or a soft sweet
1 egg
175 g marzipan (almond paste)
Paper crown for decoration

Instructions
◆ Preheat oven to 200°C/425°F.

◆ Grease some baking paper.

◆ Roll out pastry into a 20 cm round.

◆ Spread the almond paste evenly onto the pastry.

◆ Place the bean anywhere on the filling. *(On the outside edge is better, otherwise it may get sliced into many pieces!)*

◆ Beat the egg and paint around the edges of the pastry to help seal the galette.

◆ Roll out another 20 cm piece of pastry and place it over the almond filling.

◆ Press the edges together firmly to seal. Score the top layer lightly with a sharp knife. Glaze with the remaining beaten egg.

◆ Bake for 25 minutes.

◆ Serve with the crown on the top.

Ingrédients
500 g de pâte feuilletée
1 haricot sec ou un bonbon mou
1 œuf
175 g de pâte d'amande
1 couronne en papier

Instructions
◆ *Préchauffez le four à 200°C/425°F.*

◆ *Graissez du papier sulfurisé.*

◆ *Étalez la pâte sur 20 cm.*

◆ *Étalez la pâte d'amande sur la pâte feuilletée.*

◆ *Mettez le haricot n'importe où sur la pâte.*

◆ *Battez l'œuf et étalez-le avec un pinceau à l'extérieur de la pâte.*

◆ *Étalez une nouvelle pâte sur 20 cm. Placez-la sur la pâte d'amande.*

◆ *Pressez les bords ensemble. Marquez la couche supérieure. Dorez avec l'œuf.*

◆ *Faites cuire au four pendant 25 minutes.*

◆ *Servez avec la couronne au-dessus.*

La fête des Rois

Nom: Date:

Draw and label the key vocabulary for *la fête des Rois*.

Create a Recipe card in French for a *galette*.

In pairs or groups, design a PowerPoint presentation about La *fête des Rois* for your class.

Evaluate and assess each one.

Write a newspaper report in French about how you celebrate New Year.

Investigate *Epiphany* and create a mind map of how other countries celebrate.

 **And now for some RESEARCH!**

Research New Year traditions from around the world and list the key facts that you discover.

Quick quiz

◆ When does *La fête des Rois* take place?
◆ What is a *fève*?
◆ What are the origins of *La fête des Rois*?

French Festivals and Traditions KS3
© Nicolette Hannam, Michelle Williams and Brilliant Publications

La Chandeleur
Candlemas

Background information

In France, the Catholic holiday of Candlemas is on the 2nd February and it is called *La Chandeleur*. Lots of *crêpes* are eaten on this day, but it is also tradition to foretell the future. Hold a coin in one hand and the frying pan in the other, flip the *crêpe* and if you manage to catch it in the pan, your family will be prosperous for the rest of the year.

This holiday is known as *La Chandeleur* – the Feast of Candles. In the past people used to light candles to celebrate. Even today, people light candles in rooms around their homes to spread good luck.

But today people eat pancakes as well!

Teaching ideas

◆ Buy ready made *crêpes* from the supermarket, heat and top with different fillings for the pupils to sample.

Popular toppings in France

Crêpe au jambon	Pancake with ham
Crêpe au fromage	Pancake with cheese
Crêpe à la confiture	Pancake with jam
Crêpe à la pomme	Pancake with apple
Crêpe au sucre	Pancake with sugar

Vocabulaire	
une crêpe	a pancake
un œuf	an egg
le lait	milk
la farine	flour
le beurre	butter
le sucre	sugar
un saladier	a bowl

◆ Pupils could draw pictures of these pancakes and label them in French.

◆ Pupils could mime making a pancake as you describe the actions in French (see recipe on page 14).

◆ Find out some facts about *La Chandeleur* (or Candlemas), using the Internet for help and ideas. Tell the class about what you have found out.

◆ Make crêpes using the recipe on page 14.

Crêpes

Ingredients

190 g flour
375 ml whole milk
2 large eggs
45 g sugar
a little salt
75 g unsalted butter, melted

Instructions

◆ Put the sieve on top of the bowl.

◆ Put the flour in the sieve and into the bowl.

◆ Add a little salt.

◆ Put two eggs in another bowl. Mix.

◆ Put the milk in the bowl with the eggs.

◆ Put the eggs and the milk in the bowl with the flour. Add the sugar.

◆ Mix.

◆ Add the melted butter.

◆ Mix again and start cooking!

◆ Bon appetit!

Ingrédients

190 g de farine
375 ml de lait entier
2 gros œufs
45 g de sucre
une pincée de sel
75 g de beurre doux (fondu)

Instructions

◆ *Mettez le tamis au-dessus du saladier.*

◆ *Mettez la farine dans le tamis et dans le saladier.*

◆ *Ajoutez une pincée de sel.*

◆ *Mettez deux œufs dans un autre saladier. Mélangez.*

◆ *Mettez le lait dans le saladier avec les œufs.*

◆ *Mettez les œufs et le lait dans le saladier avec la farine. Ajoutez le sucre.*

◆ *Mélangez.*

◆ *Ajoutez le beurre (fondu).*

◆ *Mélangez encore et commencez à cuire les crêpes.*

◆ *Bon appétit!*

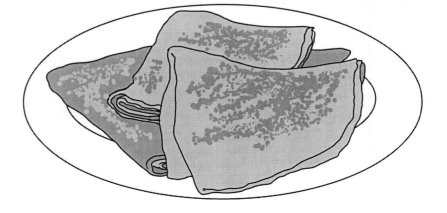

French Festivals and Traditions KS3
© Nicolette Hannam, Michelle Williams and Brilliant Publications

La Chandeleur

Nom: Date:

Design a recipe card in French for crêpes, complete with some suggested toppings.

Write a letter or email to a French friend telling them about how you celebrate Pancake Day.

 **And now for some RESEARCH!**

Investigate and research how Pancake Day is celebrated in other countries. Use the Internet and write a list comparing and contrasting.

Quick quiz

- ◆ What does *la Chandeleur* mean?
- ◆ How is it celebrated?
- ◆ What is the relevance of a coin?
- ◆ What is the significance of candles?

La Saint-Valentin

Valentine's Day

Background information

Valentine's Day, on 14th February, is celebrated in France as in this country! People send romantic cards and presents to each other.

Here is a traditional French Valentine's Day poem:

Que l'on est si bien	It's so good to be together
Le jour de la Saint-Valentin	On Saint Valentine's Day
Près de notre bien-aimée	With the one you love.
Que l'on veut aimer.	

Teaching ideas

Words for Valentine's Day cards	
Joyeuse Saint-Valentin	Happy Valentine's Day
Cher …	Dear … (boy)
Chère ...	Dear … (girl)
Bisous	Love from

Vocabulaire

l'amour	love
l'amitié	friendship
Je t'aime	I love/like you
Je ne t'aime pas	I don't love/like you
Je t'adore	I adore you
Veux-tu m'épouser?	Will you marry me?
joyeuse Saint-Valentin	Happy Valentine's Day
cher…	dear … (boy)
chère ...	dear (girl)
bisous	love from
tu es super	you're great
sors avec moi	go out with me
Comment t'appelles-tu?	What's your name?

◆ Make *une cocotte* – a 'Chatterbox' finger game (see page 17 for instructions).

Here are some suggestions for things that could be written inside:

Je t'aime	I love/like you
Je ne t'aime pas	I don't love/like you
Je t'adore	I love you
Tu es super	You're great
Sors avec moi	Go out with me
Veux-tu m'épouser?	Will you marry me?
Comment t'appelles-tu?	What is your name?

◆ Pupils could use any French vocabulary they have learned for the words on the outside flaps, eg colours, numbers etc.

Une cocotte
A chatterbox game

How to make a chatterbox

1   Fold a square piece of paper in half vertically and horizontally, and then unfold.

2   Fold all four corners so they meet at the centre point. Turn the folded square over.

3   Fold all four new corners so they meet at the centre point.

4   Fold the top edge to meet the bottom edge, crease the fold and unfold again. Fold the right edge to meet the left one, crease and unfold.

5   Hold the chatterbox as shown. Slip the pointer finger and thumb from each hand under the square flaps at the back, pinching the folds.

6. Practise opening and closing the 'mouth' of the chatterbox.

7   Write a word on each of the four corners. Open the chatterbox up and write other words on all eight triangles, or put coloured dots. Finally, lift up the flaps and write your chosen sentences underneath each triangle. You are now ready to play!

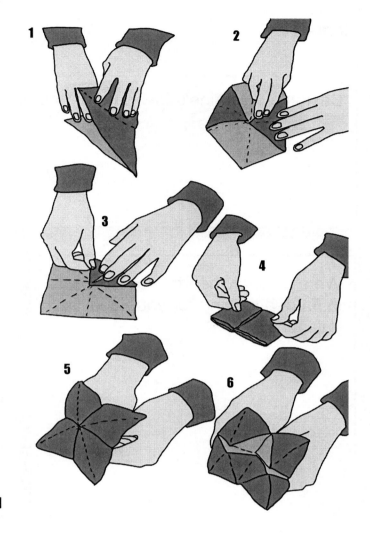

How to use a chatterbox

◆   Ask your friend to read each of the words displayed on the outside of the chatterbox and to choose one word. Spell out the word, using the French alphabet, opening and closing the chatterbox as you say each letter.

◆   At the end of spelling this word, four of the inside words, or coloured dots, will be displayed. Ask your friend to read, or name, them and to choose one.

◆   Spell out that chosen word, opening and closing the 'bird's beak' again as you say each letter. At the end of this spelling, four of the inside words will be displayed. It may be the same four words or it may be the other four words.

◆   Ask your friend to read these four words and to choose one again. Open up the chosen flap.

◆   Read out the sentence under the flap and see how your partner responds!

La Saint-Valentin

Pupil Task Sheet

  3

Nom: Date:

Design a Valentine's Day card or poster in French.

Write a 'lonely hearts' advert in French looking for your ideal Valentine.

 **And now for some RESEARCH!**

Use the Internet to find some authentic French Valentine's Day verses or poems or make up your own.

Quick quiz

◆ How is Valentine's Day celebrated in France?
◆ What is the French word for Valentine's Day?
◆ How do you say 'I love you' in French?

French Festivals and Traditions KS3
© *Nicolette Hannam, Michelle Williams and Brilliant Publications*

Mardi gras
Carnival Time

Background information
Mardi gras, or Shrove Tuesday, is an annual celebration. It is also called, *le carnaval* or Carnival Time.

The traditional colours of Mardi gras are:

French	English	Symbolising
Le violet	purple	justice
Le doré	gold	power
Le vert	green	faith

The colours originate from 1872 when the Grand Duke Alexis Romanoff of Russia visited New Orleans. It is believed that he went to find an actress called Lydia Thompson. During his stay he was asked to select the official Mardi gras colours. These colours are still used all around the world today.

An official Mardi gras flag is flown during Carnival season outside the homes of past Carnival Kings and Queens.

Origins
Mardi gras has its origins some time in the 2nd Century. During mid-February the ancient Romans would observe *'Lupercalia',* a circus type festival quite similar to the Mardi gras celebrations of today. From Rome, celebrations spread all over Europe.

In French, Mardi gras literally means 'Fat Tuesday'. This is because it falls on the day before Ash Wednesday, the last day prior to Lent, a 40-day period of fasting which ends on Easter Sunday.

The word *carnaval* comes from the Latin 'take off the flesh'. People would make the most of eating fatty foods before fasting for Lent began. You were also supposed to make fun of everything and everyone during this time, hidden behind a mask or disguise!

The slogan for Mardi gras is, '*Laissez les bons temps rouler*' translated, 'Let the good times roll'.

One of the biggest Mardi gras celebrations in France is held in Nice. People line the streets in carnival costumes and there are many floats decorated with flowers and street processions.

Records show that in the year 1294, the Comte de Provence Charles II, Duc d'Anjou began taking his holidays in Nice to join in with the Carnival celebrations. There were masked balls, masquerades, bonfires, jugglers, mimes and much more – all you needed to participate was a costume and a mask. Celebrations hit a high note in the late 19th Century at a time called the 'Belle Époque', before the World Wars.

Teaching ideas

◆ Design a Mardi gras float for a street party.

◆ Design your Mardi gras costume in the official colours. Draw and label the costume.

◆ Make an invitation to a Mardi gras party.

> Invitation de Lisa
>
> Tu es invité(e) à une fête pour Mardi gras!
>
> Rejoins-moi à ...
> Date:
> Heure:
> Lieu:

Vocabulaire

un carnaval	a carnival
laissez les bons temps rouler	let the good times roll
un bal masqué	a costume ball
un char	a float
un costume	a costume
un défilé	a parade
un feu (de joie)	a bonfire
un masque	a mask
une reine	a queen
un roi	a king
une invitation	an invitation
rejoins-moi à	join me at
la date	date
l'heure	time
le lieu	place

Mardi gras

Nom: Date:

Make up a list of questions in French you would ask someone who had been at a Mardi gras celebration. In pairs conduct interviews.

Work in teams and design a PowerPoint presentation about Mardi gras for your class. Evaluate each one and nominate a class winner!

And now for some RESEARCH!

Use the Internet to find out how Mardi gras is celebrated around the world. Make notes. Draw on film clips, sound files and photos and your own research to enter key information about this event in a grid.

Quick quiz

- ◆ What are the traditional colours for Mardi gras ?
- ◆ Can you remember what they symbolize?
- ◆ What are the origins of Mardi gras?
- ◆ How is Mardi gras celebrated in France?

Poisson d'avril

April Fool's Day

Background information

In France, on the 1st of April, pupils stick paper fish to the backs of other people for a joke. When the fish is discovered, they shout '*Poisson d'avril!*' (April fish). They also play practical jokes, like we do in the United Kingdom.

Some believe that April Fool's Day originated in France. April 1st was the beginning of the new year according to the pre-Gregorian calendar. When the Gregorian calendar was introduced, the new year's celebrations changed to January 1st. Those people who resisted the date change and still celebrated on the first of April were known as '*Poisson d'avril*' and people would play practical jokes on them.

Here are some French 'toc, toc' (knock, knock) jokes.

Toc, toc,	*Knock, knock*
Qui est là?	*Who's there?*
Anni	*Anni*
Anni qui?	*Anni who?*
Anniversaire.	*Anniversaire (birthday)*

Toc, toc	*Knock, knock*
Qui est là?	*Who's there?*
Sam.	*Sam*
Sam qui?	*Sam who?*
Samedi.	*Samedi (Saturday)*

Teaching ideas

◆ Make up your own 'Toc, toc' joke.

◆ Make a poster of your 'Toc, toc' joke.

◆ Make some paper fish to stick on people and write some key vocabulary for 'Poisson d'avril' on them.

◆ Investigate the significance of using 'fish' for April Fool's Day.

Vocabulaire

le poisson d'avril	April Fish (Fools)
un poisson	a fish
toc, toc	knock, knock
Qui est là?	Who's there?
l'anniversaire	birthday
samedi	Saturday

French Festivals and Traditions KS3
© Nicolette Hannam, Michelle Williams and Brilliant Publications

Poisson d'avril

Nom: Date:

In pairs, make up your own 'Toc, toc' joke in French and practise with your partner.

In groups, write a short play in French, where an April Fool's Day trick is played and act it out.

And now for some RESEARCH!

Use the Internet to investigate how April Fool's Day is celebrated in different countries.

Quick quiz

◆ How do French children celebrate *Poisson d'avril*?

◆ What does 'Toc, toc …' mean?

Pâques

Easter

Background information

On the Thursday before Good Friday (*vendredi saint*), all the church bells in France stop ringing. Children are told that the bell's chimes have flown back to Rome to see the Pope. On Easter morning, the bells ring again in celebration.

In France on Easter morning, children search for their Easter eggs (*les œufs de Pâques*) in the garden. Parents tell their children that the Easter eggs have come from Rome along with the chimes from the bells.

In France, traditionally it was the bells that brought Easter eggs, but nowadays children are often told that the Easter bunny (*le lapin de Pâques*) has brought them.

As in the United Kingdom, lamb is eaten for the traditional Easter meal.

Teaching ideas

◆ Write a letter or email to your French friend telling them how you celebrate Easter.

Words for Easter cards	
Joyeuses Pâques	Happy Easter
Cher …	Dear … (boy)
Chère …	Dear … (girl)
Bisous	Love from

◆ Make a treasure map. Write instructions in French for how to find the eggs.

◆ Hold a 'Decorate an Egg' competition. (Use either hard boiled eggs or pictures of eggs).

◆ Design, or make, *un bonnet de Pâques* (an Easter bonnet).

Vocabulaire

Joyeuses Pâques	Happy Easter
un œuf de Pâques	Easter egg
le lapin de Pâques	Easter bunny
un poussin	a chick
un agneau	a lamb
un panier	a basket
une église	a church
une croix	a cross
cher …	dear … (boy)
chère …	dear … (girl)
bisous	kisses
Tu veux jouer?	Would you like to play?
à ton tour	your turn
à mon tour	my turn
tu gagnes	you win
je gagne	I win
le début	start
la fin	finish
avance de X cases	move forward X spaces
recule de X cases	move back X spaces
un bonnet	a bonnet

Design 'la chasse aux œufs' - an Easter Egg Hunt game

Design an Easter Egg Hunt game and play with a friend. See if you can play speaking just in French! These words and phrases will help you:

Would you like to play?	Tu veux jouer?
Your turn.	À ton tour.
My turn.	À mon tour.
You win.	Tu gagnes.
I win.	Je gagne.
Start	Le début
Finish	La fin
Throw the dice.	Lance le dé.
Move forward 3 spaces.	Avance de 3 cases.
Move back 3 spaces.	Recule de 3 cases.

Pâques

Nom: Date:

Make an Easter card in French and a list of key Easter words.

Working in teams, design a French Easter Egg Hunt board game. Play each other's games and evaluate. Nominate a class winner.

And now for some RESEARCH!

In pairs or groups, research how Easter is celebrated in other countries. Choose a country and share your findings with the rest of the class.

Quick quiz

- ◆ How do you say 'Happy Easter' in French?
- ◆ What is the significance of the 'bells'?
- ◆ What do French children do on Easter morning?

French Festivals and Traditions KS3
© Nicolette Hannam, Michelle Williams and Brilliant Publications

Les contes de fées
Fairy stories

Background information

In Paris around 1700, French authors were some of the first to start recording oral stories that have now developed into the fairy tale genre. They were originally aimed at adults. Charles Perrault was the first to write down Red Riding Hood and Sleeping Beauty. He also wrote Cinderella and Puss in Boots.

The Brothers Grimm are very famous German authors in the fairy tale genre. They first recorded Snow White and the Seven Dwarfs. All of these tales, and many more, are now known around the world as magical stories for children. In England, they also take the form of pantomime.

The French term '*Les contes de fées*' originates from Madame d'Aulnoy. She was a French writer who wrote fairy tales towards the end of the 17th century. She published two fairy tale collections, which were sadly regarded as mere entertainment by both France and England.

In France, children read and learn fairy stories, just like children all over the world.

Here are some titles of fairy tales in French:

Le petit chaperon rouge	Little Red Riding Hood
La Belle au bois dormant	Sleeping Beauty
Blanche-Neige et les sept nains	Snow White and the Seven Dwarfs
La belle et la bête	Beauty and the Beast
Le Chat Botté	Puss in Boots
Cendrillon	Cinderella

Teaching ideas

◆ Read a simple fairy tale for the pupils to act out. Familiarize them with the key vocabulary first. Display the fairy tale for the pupils to follow as you read it aloud.

◆ Ask the pupils to respond with physical gestures when they hear key words or character's names. Use lots of repetition.

◆ Use a simple French fairy tale in a sequencing activity. Jumble up key sentences for the pupils to reorder.

◆ Rewrite the ending of a familiar fairy story and vote for the best one!

◆ Ask the pupils to pretend to be a character, for example Red Riding Hood. What could we ask her? Pupils could ask them their name/age/favourite colour, and so on.

Vocabulaire

Il était une fois …	Once upon a time …
le roi	the king
la reine	the queen
la princesse	the princess
le prince	the prince
la fée	the fairy
la marraine	fairy godmother
la forêt	the forest
un bois	a wood
le palais	the palace
le loup	the wolf
la grand-mère	grandma
les sept nains	the seven dwarfs
la baguette magique	a magic wand
la bête	the beast
le monstre	the monster
le bûcheron	the woodcutter
le château	the castle
la sorcière	the wicked witch
les sœurs	the ugly sisters
une citrouille	a pumpkin
une pantoufle de verre	a glass slipper
la souris	the mouse
Miroir, miroir joli, qui est la plus belle au pays?	Mirror, mirror on the wall, who is the fairest of them all?

◆ Can the pupils use simple French to change the beginning or the ending of the story? They could be given a choice of two endings, in French, that they have to translate and choose.

◆ What story do you think this rhyme comes from?

Miroir, miroir joli   Mirror, mirror on the wall
Qui est la plus belle   Who is the fairest
au pays?   of them all?

◆ Pupils could match French characters names and key words to French fairy tale titles. Suggested answers are in the chart below:

Le petit chaperon rouge (Little Red Riding Hood)	La Belle au bois dormant (Sleeping Beauty)	Cendrillon (Cinderella)	Le Chat Botté (Puss in Boots)
Le petit chaperon rouge	La Belle au bois dormant	Cendrillon	Le Chat Botté
Le loup (the wolf)	Le prince (Prince)	Les deux sœurs (the two ugly sisters)	Le palais (palace)
La grand-mère (Grandma)	Le château (castle)	Le prince (Prince)	Le roi (King)
Le bûcheron (the woodcutter)	Les fées (Fairies)	La marraine (Fairy Godmother)	La souris (mouse)
	La sorcière (wicked witch)	Une citrouille (a pumpkin)	
		Une pantoufle de verre (a glass slipper)	

◆ Use the Red Riding Hood dialogue on page 30. Pupils could act it out in assembly. Or each phrase could be given to the pupils to match to a character. A translation is given below (LPCR = Le petit chaperon rouge):

(LPCR meets the wolf in the forest.)

LPCR: Bonjour. Je m'appelle le   Hello. My name is Little Red Riding Hood.
     petit chaperon rouge.   I am 6 years old. I am an only child.
     J'ai six ans. Je suis fille unique.

Le loup: Bonjour ma petite.   Hello little one. What are you doing here?
     Que fais-tu ici?

LPCR: Ma grand-mère est malade.   My grandmother is ill. She lives in the forest.
     Elle habite dans la forêt.

(The wolf goes to Grandma's house, dressed as LPCR.)

French Festivals and Traditions KS3
© Nicolette Hannam, Michelle Williams and Brilliant Publications

Le loup:	Bonjour grand-mère.	Hello, Grandma.
Grand-mère:	Bonjour chaperon rouge. Ça va?	Hello, Little Red Riding Hood. How are you?
Le loup:	Super, merci. Et toi, grand-mère?	Super, thanks. And you, Grandma?
Grand-mère:	Ça va mal, ma petite.	I am ill, little one.

(The wolf eats Grandma and disguises himself as her).

LPCR:	Salut grand-mère. C'est moi, chaperon rouge.	Hi Grandma. It's me, Little Red Riding Hood.
Le loup:	Salut. Entre, ma petite.	Hi. Enter, little one.
LPCR:	Oh, grand-mère, comme tu as de grands yeux!	Oh Grandma, what big eyes you have!
Le loup:	C'est pour mieux te voir!	All the better to see you with.
LPCR:	Oh, grand-mère, comme tu as de grandes oreilles!	Oh Grandma, what big ears you have!
Le loup:	C'est pour mieux t'entendre!	All the better to hear you with.
LPCR:	Oh, grand-mère, comme tu as une grande bouche … et de grandes dents!	Oh Grandma, what a big mouth you have … and what big teeth!
Le loup:	C'est pour mieux te manger!	All the better to eat you with!
LPCR:	Au secours!	Help!

(The woodcutter runs in the house and saves LPCR – and cuts open wolf's stomach to save Grandma.)

LPCR & grand-mère:	Merci beaucoup, Monsieur.	Thank you very much, Sir.
La fin		*The end*

Le petit chaperon rouge

(LPCR meets the wolf in the forest.)

LPCR: Bonjour. Je m'appelle le petit chaperon rouge. J'ai six ans. Je suis fille unique.

Le loup: Bonjour ma petite. Que fais-tu ici?

LPCR: Ma grand-mère est malade. Elle habite dans la forêt.

(The wolf goes to Grandma's house, dressed as LPCR.)

Le loup: Bonjour grand-mère.

Grand-mère: Bonjour chaperon rouge. Ça va?

Le loup: Super, merci. Et toi, grand-mère?

Grand-mère: Ça va mal, ma petite.

(The wolf eats Grandma and disguises himself as her).

LPCR: Salut grand-mère. C'est moi, chaperon rouge.

Le loup: Salut. Entre, ma petite.

LPCR: Oh, grand-mère, comme tu as de grands yeux!

Le loup: C'est pour mieux te voir!

LPCR: Oh, grand-mère, comme tu as de grandes oreilles!

Le loup: C'est pour mieux t'entendre!

LPCR: Oh, grand-mère, comme tu as une grande bouche … et de grandes dents!

Le loup: C'est pour mieux te manger!

LPCR: Au secours!

(The woodcutter runs in the house and saves LPCR – and cuts open wolf's stomach to save Grandma.)

LPCR &
grand-mère: Merci beaucoup, Monsieur.

La fin

French Festivals and Traditions KS3
© Nicolette Hannam, Michelle Williams and Brilliant Publications

Les contes de fées

7

Nom: Date:

Plan and present your own fairy tale in French. Give your story a modern twist – make it a story for a newspaper.

Using the Little Red Riding Hood story work in pairs to construct as many sentences in French as you can which reflect the storyline. In groups evaluate and improve your sentences.

And now for some RESEARCH!

Investigate and research the Brothers Grimm. List key facts about them and present to the rest of the class.

Quick quiz

◆ Who were the famous brothers who wrote fairy tales?

◆ Can you name any fairy tales – in French?

La fête du travail

May Day/Labour Day

Background information

May Day traditions go back to the beginning of time. In ancient times, it was the date when sailors went back to sea, and in the Middle Ages, May was when betrothals were made.

The 1st May has been a public holiday in France since 1889. Nowadays there are many street processions and parties.

La fête du travail translates as 'Work Party' but means 'Workers' Day'. Historically 1st May was the beginning of union activities, remembering previous successes that had been fought and won for French workers. For those not taking part in celebrations and marches, it is a day to spend as a family.

A bouquet of lily of the valley, or *un petit bouquet de muguet*, is an essential part of May Day in France. It has been associated with French May Day celebrations since the Renaissance and is thought to bring good luck.

On the 1st May, or 'Lily of the Valley Day', you give a bunch of lilies to close family members (eg parents, children, grandmother, etc) as a sign of your affection.

Teaching ideas

◆   Can you find a picture of some lily of the valley?

◆   What could you do, or give, as a sign of your affection? Who would you give it to? Can you explain why?

Vocabulaire

la fête du travail	May Day/Labour Day
un petit bouquet de muguet	a small bouquet of lily of the valley
un ami/une amie	a friend

La fête du travail

8

Nom: Date:

Organize a party for May day. Design posters and invitations in French.

Make menus and a list of activities for your May Day Party.

And now for some RESEARCH!

Research to compare and contrast how May Day is celebrated in France and in Britain. Present your findings.

Quick quiz

◆ What are the origins of *la fête du travail*?
◆ What is the significance of Lily of the Valley?
◆ What is Lily of the Valley called in French?

La fête des Mères

Mother's Day

Background information

Mother's Day in France was inaugurated by Napoleon and made an official holiday in 1950. It takes place on the last Sunday in May, except when this is Whit Sunday. Then Mother's Day is deferred to the first Sunday of June. So in France Mother's Day isn't in March, like in the United Kingdom.

It is celebrated in the same way as we celebrate, giving cards and presents. Often children give flowers. Sometimes children write short poems for their mother. Often families have a big lunch together.

Mother's Day is celebrated on different days throughout the world. Here are the dates for some other French-speaking countries:

2nd Sunday in June	Luxembourg
2nd Sunday in May	Belgium, Canada, Switzerland
21st March (equinox)	Morocco
Last Sunday in May	Algeria, Tunisia

Teaching ideas

◆ Share this poem with the class:

Celle que l'on aime	She's the person you love the most
Et qui est la plus belle,	And she's the most beautiful,
C'est notre maman.	She's our mum.

◆ Use the poem to look at adjectives. Brainstorm more descriptive adjectives.

◆ Design a '*Diplôme de la meilleure maman*' – a certificate for the best mum.

◆ Draw and describe your mum in French.

◆ Write a persuasive letter explaining why your mum is the best in the whole world.

◆ Write a newspaper article about your mum winning an award.

Vocabulaire

la fête des Mères	Mother's Day
à	to
de	from
Ma chère Maman	Dear Mum
Je t'aime	I love you
chère	dear (girl)
bisous	love from
bonne fête Maman	Happy Mother's Day
la meilleure mère	the best mum
un diplôme	a certificate

*Diplôme
de la
Meilleure Maman
attribué à*

_____

La fête des Mères

9

Nom: Date:

Design a Mother's Day card in French.

Make up a Mother's Day rhyme or poem in French.

And now for some RESEARCH!

Research the origins of Mother's Day and how it is celebrated in other countries. Write a list of the key information and present to the class.

Quick quiz

◆ When does Mother's Day take place in France?
◆ How is this different to in Britain?
◆ How is it celebrated in France?

Joyeux anniversaire

Happy Birthday

Background information

In France, when it is your birthday, all your family gathers to wish you a Happy Birthday, which in French is '*joyeux anniversaire!*'

Then, you eat a very big cake, usually made of chocolate. On the cake, you have candles according to your age. Then, all the family sings '*joyeux anniversaire*' – 'Happy Birthday to you!' They use the same tune as we do.

After eating the cake, your family gives you presents and cards.

Note: when writing *Joyeux Anniversaire* and *Bonne Fête* on cards you use capital letters, but normally they aren't capitalized.

Some popular French names

Boy's Names	English equivalent	Girl's Names	English equivalent
Olivier	Oliver	Lucie	Lucy
Pierre	Peter	Nathalie	Natalie
Guillaume	William	Charlotte	Charlotte
Jacques	James	Laure	Laura
Jean	John	Noémie	Naomie
Luc	Luke	Sophia	Sophie

Saints days

In France, in common with many other predominantly Roman Catholic countries, people have Saint's days as well as birthdays. Traditionally, in France, children were given the name of the Saint on whose special day they were born. Nowadays people prefer to choose their children's names, but the tradition of having a Saint's day is still kept, so now people have two days to celebrate: their Birthday and their Saint's day. For example, if your name is Luc, then in addition to your birthday, you would celebrate your Saint's day, 18th October. On your Saint's day people will say to you *bonne fête!* – 'Happy Saint's Day!' Some days have more than one saint associated with it. The list below shows some of the Saint's days for June (*juin*).

1	Justin	11	Barnabé	21	Rodolphe
2	Blandine	12	Guy	22	Alban
3	Kévin	13	Antoine	23	Audrey
4	Clotilde	14	Elisée	24	Jean-Baptiste
5	Igor	15	Germaine	25	Prosper
6	Norbert	16	Jean-François Regis	26	Anthelme
7	Gilbert	17	Hervé	27	Fernand
8	Médard	18	Léonce	28	Irénée
9	Diane	19	Romuald	29	Pierre/Paul
10	Landry	20	Silvère	30	Martial

Carte d'identité

Everyone in France has a national identity card (*Carte nationale d'identité sécurisée* or CNIS). It is an official non-compulsory identity document consisting of a laminated plastic card bearing a photograph, name and date of birth.

They are valid for a period of 10 years and are issued free of charge.

Teaching ideas

◆ Design your own ID card (*carte d'identité*), with the following information on it:

Nom:	Name:
Date de naissance:	Date of Birth:
Âge:	Age:
Domicile:	Where you live:
Famille:	Family:
Cheveux:	Hair:
Yeux:	Eyes:
Taille:	Height:
Passe-temps:	Hobbies:

◆ Sing '*joyeux anniversaire*' – to the tune of 'Happy Birthday to You':

> Joyeux anniversaire,
> Joyeux anniversaire,
> Joyeux anniversaire (name),
> Joyeux anniversaire!

◆ Do a birthday survey (*un sondage*) to find out in which month people in your class have their birthday, in French.

Quelle est la date de ton anniversaire?
Mon anniversaire est le ...

Nom	Anniversaire
Mme Williams	20 juin
Luc	17 avril

Vocabulaire

la carte d'identité	ID card
le nom	name
la date de naissance	date of birth
l'âge	age
le domicile	where you live
la famille	family
les cheveux	hair
les yeux	eyes
la taille	height
les passe-temps	hobbies
joyeux anniversaire	Happy Birthday
bonne fête	Happy Saint's Day
un sondage	a survey
Quelle est le date de ton anniversaire?	When is your birthday?
Mon anniversaire est le ...	My birthday is ...

Joyeux anniversaire

Nom: Date:

Design a French Birthday card and invitation to your party. Make a list of presents you would like to receive in French.

Look at the French names on page 36, work out how to pronounce them. Compare and contrast with popular names in Britain.

And now for some RESEARCH!

Research the origins of Saints Days and work out when yours is.

Quick quiz

◆ How do you say 'Happy Birthday' in French?
◆ Why do you have two birthdays in France?
◆ How do French people celebrate their birthdays?

Le festival de Cannes
Cannes Film Festival

Background information

Cannes is a city in the South of France. It is one of the best-known cities of the French Riviera and is famous for expensive, glitzy hotels, fast cars and celebrities. The city hosts many famous events, including *Le festival de Cannes* (the annual Cannes Film Festival). It is an annual festival which takes place in May or June.

In 1939, the French Minister for the Arts proposed the creation of an International Film Festival event in France. Cannes was chosen for its 'sunshine and enchanting setting.' The first festival was postponed due to the war so 1946 saw the very first International Film Festival. The festival has evolved and now has a series of initiatives encouraging both professional and creative development.

The Cannes Film Festival is widely publicized all over the world and attracts famous celebrities, writers, producers, directors and musicians to showcase their films. It is also famous for its 'red carpet' and the outfits and jewellery worn by the celebrities!

Teaching ideas

◆ What would you wear to this famous festival? Design an outfit.

◆ Use a digital DVD recorder to make a short film of your own, based on a topic you like. Work in groups to plan your script and decide who will do what. Then show the finished DVDs to the rest of the class.

◆ Write a newspaper report based on the Cannes Film Festival. Who is there? Which films are showing? Who is going to the after parties?

◆ Find Cannes on a map of France and plot your journey there, from home.

Vocabulaire

un film	a film
un acteur	an actor
une actrice	an actress
un directeur	a director
un producteur	a producer
un tapis rouge	a red carpet
un musicien	a musician
une célébrité	a celebrity
C'était étonnant!	It was amazing!
J'ai adoré!	I loved it!
Cinq étoiles!	Five stars!

Le festival de Cannes

Nom: Date:

Make up some questions in French you would ask a famous person. In pairs conduct an interview, using your questions.

Create a brochure in French about Cannes.

And now for some RESEARCH!

Research Cannes using the Internet, film clips, sound files and photos. List the key information in French. Present this information to the class and evaluate each other's work.

Quick quiz

- ◆ Where is Cannes?
- ◆ What happens here?
- ◆ What do you know about this festival?
- ◆ What are the origins of this festival?

French Festivals and Traditions KS3
© Nicolette Hannam, Michelle Williams and Brilliant Publications

Le quatorze juillet

14th July

Background information

The 14th July is Bastille Day in France, the French National Day. It dates back to 1789 and the fall of the Bastille prison to the Revolutionaries.

It is a bank holiday and many people celebrate with a street party and fireworks. There is a military parade on the Champs-Elysées in Paris. A huge flag is flown from the Arc de Triomphe.

The Bastille was a prison in which kings and queens used to lock up prisoners, often unfairly. On 14th July 1789, a large group of French people gathered together to storm the Bastille and show that the monarchy did not have all the power.

The prisoners were released, and the King and Queen were imprisoned with their children in Paris. The King, Louis XVI, and his wife Marie-Antoinette were sent to their death by guillotine in 1793. The children were sent back to Marie-Antoinette's family in Austria. The monarchy had ended and democracy had begun.

Symbols of France

Le tricolore

Le tricolore is the French flag. It was first used in 1789, after the French Revolution. It was officially adopted as the French national flag on 15th February 1794. The colours represent those of Paris (blue and red), combined with that of the Bourbon Dynasty (white), though they are usually associated with freedom, equality, and brotherhood (fraternity), the ideals of the French Revolution.

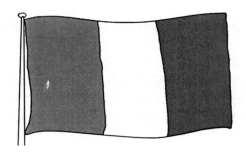

Marianne

Marianne is a national emblem of France. She represents the spirit and values of France, specifically Liberty and Reason. She can be seen in many places in France, often in town halls and law courts. There is a large bronze statue of her in Paris. She is also on one of the sculptures on the Arc de Triomphe, victoriously leading the French army. Her profile is also on stamps, and was on the former Franc coins and bank notes.

Marianne wears a special hat called a 'Phrygian cap'. Freed slaves wore it in Roman times. The hat soon became a symbol of freedom. Marianne came to represent the French Republic during the French Revolution in 1789, wearing the 'cap of Liberty'. People began wearing red caps to symbolize that they were fighting for freedom.

Marianne's name was chosen during the French Revolution because it was the most common name at the time.

During this century her features have been modelled on famous beautiful female actors. In 2000 the Mayors of France voted for a new Marianne, and the actress Laetitia Casta was chosen. Then, in 2005, a decision was made not to use a real woman as the ideal for Marianne. The latest design incorporates North African features to represent the ethnic cultures that reside in France.

The logo of the French government combines Marianne with the colours of the French flag.

La Marseillaise

The French national anthem was composed in one night during the French Revolution by Claude-Joseph Rouget de Lisle, a captain of the engineers and amateur musician stationed in Strasbourg in 1792. It was played at a patriotic banquet at Marseille, and copies were given to the revolutionary forces who sang it as they marched into Paris.

The anthem became known as the La Marseillaise because it was popular with volunteer army units from Marseille. It became the French national anthem in 1795. La Marseillaise was banned and reinstated several times because of its revolutionary associations. It has been the national anthem of France since it was last reinstated in 1879.

Le coq gaulois

Le coq gaulois, the Gallic Rooster, has become a sporting symbol for France. It all began as a joke in Roman Times when France was known as Gaul. The Latin word '*Gallus*' was used to describe a person living in Gaul, but it also translates as rooster. So the rooster began to represent French people, and the tradition has survived over two thousand years.

The Gallic Rooster was used to represent France by Kings in the Middle Ages on coins and in pictures. Napoleon tried to change the image to an eagle but the rooster returned in the 19th century on flags, and on the uniforms of The National Guard. It is on one of the gates of the Elysée Palace, the President's Official Residence.

In World War I the rooster became a symbol of courage. In the 20th century it evolved into a symbol for sport, and became the emblem for the French teams.

French Festivals and Traditions KS3
© *Nicolette Hannam, Michelle Williams and Brilliant Publications*

Teaching ideas

◆ Begin the lesson with a physical activity – marching as if you are on military parade. March with the pupils (on the spot if in the classroom). Instruct them briskly to stretch their arms, touch opposite knee and so on. Give instructions in French, and allow the pupils to copy your actions:

Levez-vous	Stand up
Asseyez-vous	Sit down
Sautez	Jump
Frappez des mains	Clap your hands
Etirez-vous	Stretch
Touchez vos pieds	Touch your toes
Tournez	Turn around
Marchez	Walk
Marchez plus vite	Walk faster

Vocabulaire

Bonne Fête Nationale	Happy Bastille Day
Vive la France!	Hurrah for France!
Le tricolore	The French flag
la liberté	liberty/freedom
l'égalité	equality
la fraternité	fraternity/brotherhood
La Marseillaise	The French National Anthem
un défilé militaire	a military parade
un soldat	a soldier

◆ Discuss the meaning of the words: Liberty, Equality and Fraternity.

◆ Learn about flags around the world. Draw and colour some and label in French.

◆ Listen to the French national anthem: La Marseillaise. Examine the words in both French and English and discuss. You could compare La Marseillaise to the British national anthem.

◆ Draw and colour the image that La Marseillaise creates in your mind.

◆ Discuss symbols in the United Kingdom (see box).

Symbols of the United Kingdom

The Union Jack, and each country's flag within it (see below)

England
Symbols: the three lions, red rose (appears on the England Rugby Team kit), oak tree
Patron saint: St George (23rd April)
Flag: the red cross (cross of St George)

Scotland
Symbols: the thistle, bagpipes, tartan kilts
Patron saint: St Andrew (30th November)
Flag: white diagonal cross (called a saltire) on a blue background (cross of St Andrew)

Northern Ireland
Symbols: shamrock, harp, Celtic cross
Patron saint: St Patrick (17th March)
Flag: red diagonal cross (saltire) on a white background (cross of St Patrick)

Wales
Symbols: leeks, daffodils, red dragon.
Patron saint: St David (1st March)
Flag: red dragon on a white (top) and green (bottom) background

You could also discuss The Royal Family.

Le quatorze juillet

Nom: Date:

Imagine you are on the Champs Elysées on the 14th July. Plan and present a short talk about the celebrations.

Write a newspaper article in French dating from the 14th July 1789.

And now for some RESEARCH!

Research Bastille Day using film clips, sound files and photos. List the key information in French to present this information to the class and evaluate each other's work.

Quick quiz

- When is Bastille Day?
- What are the origins of Bastille Day?
- Name two French symbols.

French Festivals and Traditions KS3
© Nicolette Hannam, Michelle Williams and Brilliant Publications

Planning a holiday

Background information

France is the second largest country in Europe, after Russia. It is known as 'l'hexagone' (the hexagon) due to its shape. It is double the size of the United Kingdom and has a population of over 60 million people. France is bordered by water on three sides (the Channel, the Atlantic Ocean and the Mediterranean Sea) and has eight neighbouring countries (Belgium, Luxembourg, Germany, Switzerland, Italy, Monaco, Andorra and Spain). It is only 35 kms from the south coast of Britain.

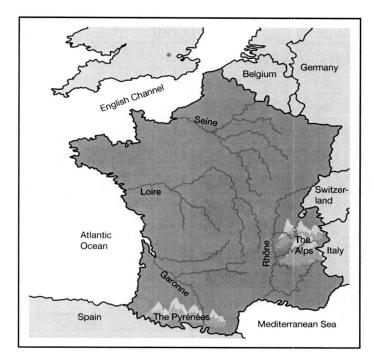

The capital of France is Paris, which has a population of just over 10 million in the centre and the surrounding suburbs. At least 20 million people visit Paris every year. The Eiffel Tower has become a symbol of France and attracts many visitors. Paris has an underground called Le métro, used by approximately five million people every day. You can take a tour of Paris using the Internet. Key 'virtual tour of Paris' into a search engine.

The highest mountain in France is Mont Blanc at 4,810 m. The longest river is the Loire at 1012 m. France has so many choices for holidays – busy cities and towns, rivers, lakes and tall mountains. The most popular place for holidaymakers is the area in the South of France bordering on the Mediterranean Sea, known as Le Midi. To the east is the French Riviera (La Côte d'Azur) with the rich towns of Monte Carlo and Cannes. To the west is the Languedoc region. Many holidaymakers choose to camp in a tent or caravan due to the warmer climate.

Tourism is great for the economy but unfortunately brings litter and pollution. Twenty-five percent of France is forest and the influx of people during holiday times brings an increased risk of forest fires.

Travelling to France

We can travel to France by ferry, aeroplane or train. Many people choose to drive to a ferry port and travel by boat so that they have their own car whilst they are abroad. Popular ferry routes are Dover to Calais, Portsmouth to Le Havre, and Poole to Cherbourg. People can eat, sleep or even go the cinema on a ferry. Flying to France is easy and quite affordable now. Popular British airports are London Heathrow, Gatwick, Stansted or Leeds Bradford. You can fly to almost every major city in France, depending on which airline you choose.

Since 1994 you can travel to France by train. The Eurotunnel is a twin tunnel built under the English Channel, linking Folkestone in England to Calais in France. You can drive on and stay in your car for the 35 minute journey. Alternatively, Eurostar trains leave for Paris from St Pancreas International Station in London several times a day, travelling through the tunnel. The trains travel at 186 mph and the journey takes 2 hours and 15 minutes.

French Festivals and Traditions KS3
© Nicolette Hannam, Michelle Williams and Brilliant Publications

Where else is French spoken?

French is an official language in 29 countries, second only to English (spoken officially in 55). French and English are the only languages spoken as a native language on five continents and the only languages taught in every country in the world.

Country	Continent
Belgium	Europe
Benin	Africa
Burkina Faso	Africa
Burundi	Africa
Cameroon	Africa
Canada	North America
Central Africa Republic	Africa
Chad	Africa
Comoros	Africa
Democratic Republic of the Congo	Africa
Ivory Coast	Africa
Djibouti	Africa
Equatorial Guinea	Africa
France	Europe
Gabon	Africa

Country	Continent
Guinea	Africa
Haiti	Caribbean
Luxembourg	Europe
Madagascar	Africa
Mali	Africa
Monaco	Europe
Niger	Africa
Republic of the Congo	Africa
Rwanda	Africa
Senegal	Africa
Seychelles	Africa
Switzerland	Europe
Togo	Africa
Vanuatu	Oceania (Asia)

French is the official language in the French overseas departments of Guadeloupe and Martinique and in the overseas collectivity of French Polynesia. French is also widely spoken in the following countries, but it is not an official language: Morocco, Algeria, Tunisia, Lebanon, Mauritania, Mauritius and Andorra.

French Festivals and Traditions KS3
© Nicolette Hannam, Michelle Williams and Brilliant Publications

Teaching ideas

◆ Look at a map of France and give the pupils some key facts about France. Make comparisons with the United Kingdom in your discussion. If you have an Interactive Whiteboard, you can find a map of France in the Gallery. If not, there are many good examples on the Internet. Discuss main towns, key geographical features and well-known landmarks.

Vocabulaire	
les vacances	holiday
le ferry	ferry
le train	train
l'avion	aeroplane
la voiture	car
voyager	to travel

◆ Pupils could pretend to be on holiday in France and write a postcard home.

◆ Pupils could plan their dream holiday to a destination of their choice. They need to think about the climate, which languages are spoken there and the activities available.

◆ Pupils could write about the best holiday they have ever had and explain why.

◆ Use weather sites on the Internet to compare weather in a locality in France, eg in the Alps or on the Côte d'Azur with that in your locality, over a period of time.

◆ The pupils could work in pairs to draw a Venn diagram, comparing France and the United Kingdom.

◆ Pupils could make a poster advertising either Britain or France as an excellent holiday destination. They should use a range of persuasive techniques (link to Literacy work).

◆ Highlight all the places on a world map where French is spoken.

◆ Do a survey to find out what other languages are spoken in the school. Locate the country/countries where these languages are spoken using maps, atlases and globes.

◆ Talk to pupils about which other languages they would like to learn and why.

Planning a holiday

13

Nom: Date:

Plan a trip to France in French. Give details of how you will travel, where you will stay, what you will do there. Present this to the class.

Design a PowerPoint presentation of the above task.

In groups, investigate and create a quiz based on geographical and demographic facts about any country.

And now for some RESEARCH!

Research an area of France and list key information about it. Design a brochure for this region. Email the tourist information centre for help and ideas.

Quick quiz

- ◆ What shape is France known as?
- ◆ Name some countries which border France.
- ◆ Which 'seas' border France?
- ◆ What is the capital city of France?
- ◆ What language is spoken?
- ◆ What is the unit of currency in France?
- ◆ Name the highest mountain in France.
- ◆ What is the South of France known as?
- ◆ Name some other countries where French is spoken.

French Festivals and Traditions KS3
© Nicolette Hannam, Michelle Williams and Brilliant Publications

How is French culture incorporated into our everyday life?

Background information

Due to the amount of travelling that now takes place across and around the world, the cultures of different countries can be transferred to new places more easily. Some people immigrate to different countries and take traditions with them. Others bring back ideas from travels and holidays.

Popular songs and films demonstrate different cultures and influence audiences. Television programmes show us places and recipes we have never seen before, and inspire us to try new things.

Large supermarkets are a great place to examine the influence of different cultures through the food that is sold. French cheese is popular, and baguettes can often be bought fresh from the in-store bakery. There is always a large section of French wine. Many towns have occasional French Markets. There is also the opportunity to sample all different types of cuisine in an ever-increasing range of restaurants in towns and cities.

In schools, pupils have the opportunity to learn about interesting and diverse religious festivals.

Teaching ideas

◆ Discuss French influences on life in the United Kingdom. Topics could include language, food, drink, music, fashion and so on.

◆ Make a mind map of the different French influences on life in the United Kingdom.

Comparing cultures

14

Nom: Date:

Compare and contrast aspects of life in France and Britain. Discuss.

Make a PowerPoint presentation depicting examples of how aspects of French culture are incorporated into British life.

And now for some RESEARCH!

Investigate how other countries influence life in Britain. Present your findings to the class.

Quick quiz
◆   Name some typical French food and drinks.
◆   Do you know the names of any famous French people?

French Festivals and Traditions KS3
© Nicolette Hannam, Michelle Williams and Brilliant Publications

La rentrée
A new school year

Background information

La rentrée is when everything in France 'gets back to normal'. Adults return to work, and children to school after the long August holidays. It literally translates as 're-entry'. Pupils begin their new school year.

A typical school day in France

Children in France start nursery school (*l'école maternelle*) at 3 years old. They stay all day and begin to learn how to read and write. When they are six they move to primary school (*l'école primaire*). They start to learn a foreign language – often English. At the age of eleven they move to secondary school (*le collège*). The days are long, from about 8.30 am until 4.30 pm, but include a two-hour lunch break. Pupils do not wear uniforms.

French children used not to go to school on Wednesday afternoons and had lessons on Saturday mornings instead. However, this is changing. Now school on Saturday mornings is less common. Some children do not have school on Wednesday either, but most go on Wednesday mornings. As a consequence, some of the school holidays have been shortened.

In France a lot of teaching time is devoted to the teaching of handwriting (see example on page 54). Huge importance is placed on excellent presentation. A uniform style of handwriting is taught throughout primary school and pupils must practise continually until they can write as expected.

In French schools, everyone has a school dinner. Packed lunches do not exist. Children sit down to a three-course meal. They all eat the same dishes; there are no choices. The first course (*l'entrée*) is often soup, salad or melon. The main course (*le plat principal*) will usually be meat or fish served with rice, pasta or couscous and vegetables. The dessert (*le dessert*) is usually fresh fruit, yoghurt, or sometimes, cake. Cheese is usually available too. There is always lots of bread, and the children drink water. Schools work hard to provide children with a healthy, balanced meal.

The organization of the academic system in France

L'école primaire (primary school)

	UK equivalent	Age
CP	Year 2	6–7
CE1	Year 3	7–8
CE2	Year 4	8–9
CM1	Year 5	9–10
CM2	Year 6	10–11

CP = Cours Préparatoire
CE = Cours Elémentaire
CM = Cours Moyen

Le collège (secondary school up to GCSE level)

	UK equivalent	Age
6ème	Year 7	11–12
5ème	Year 8	12–13
4ème	Year 9	13–14
3ème	Year 10	14–15

At the end of 3ème, pupils take an exam called 'Le Brevet – Brevet Elémentaire de Premier Cycle'.

Le lycée (equivalent to sixth form college)

	UK equivalent	Age
Seconde	Year 11	15–16
Première	Year 12	16–17
Terminale	Year 13	17–18

At the end of Première, pupils take the first part of the 'Baccalauréat exam'.

At the end of Terminale, pupils take the final part of the 'Baccalauréat exam'.

In France, it is compulsory to go the school until the age of 16.

Teaching ideas

◆ Revise school subjects.

◆ Pupils could design a brochure in French to welcome newcomers to their year group next September.

◆ Pupils could think about their first day at school, in a new school year. How did they feel? What did they do? Discuss.

◆ You could display a typical timetable in French and ask pupils questions. Which lesson is first in the morning? Which lesson comes after French? Which lesson is last on Friday afternoon? Quelle est ta matière préférée? Practise tense work.

◆ Pupils could revise the French names of the fruit and vegetables they have learned as a link to healthy eating. Make vocabulary lists for these.

◆ Pupils could decorate a typical French school menu, drawing a picture of each dish. The audience could be French pupils.

Vocabulaire

l'école maternelle	nursery school
l'école primaire	primary school
le collège	secondary school
le lycée	equivalent to sixth form college
la cantine	the canteen
Qu'est-ce-que tu aimes manger?	What do you like to eat?
l'entrée	starter
le plat principal	the main meal
le dessert	dessert
les mathématiques	maths
les sciences	science
le sport	PE
le français	French
l'anglais	English
le dessin	art
l'histoire	history
la géographie	geography
la musique	music
la technologie	ICT/computers

Menu

Entrée	**Starter**
½ pamplemousse avec du sucre	Half grapefruit with sugar
Plat principal	**Main course**
Bœuf braisé sauce brune	Beef braised in gravy
Purée de brocolis	Pureed broccoli
Le fromage	Cheese
La salade	Salad
Dessert	**Dessert**
Fruit de saison	Fresh fruit of the season
Flan au chocolat	Chocolate flan

◆ Pupils could list food they do and do not like in French and give reasons why and why not.

L'alphabet français

L'Alphabet

A	a	K	k	U	u
B	b	L	l	V	v
C	c	M	m	W	w
D	d	N	n	X	x
E	e	O	o	Y	y
F	f	P	p	Z	z
G	g	Q	q		
H	h	R	r		
I	i	S	s		
J	j	T	t		

French Festivals and Traditions KS3
© Nicolette Hannam, Michelle Williams and Brilliant Publications

La rentrée

Nom: Date:

Plan and design a PowerPoint presentation in French depicting your typical school day.

Email or write a letter to a French friend asking them questions (in French) about their daily routine.

 **And now for some RESEARCH!**

Research school lunches in France. Visit a French school website and find out what they are having for lunch. List key information and design a school menu in French.

Quick quiz

◆ What is *la rentrée*?
◆ Name some differences between French and British schools.
◆ How are lunch times different?

Comparing pastimes and everyday life

Background information

French children have similar hobbies to British children. Perhaps, due to the warmer climate, French children may spend more time outdoors. Everyday life is also very similar. School days may differ slightly (eg children do not wear uniform to school). The most beneficial way to compare everyday life is to show video clips of French children to begin discussions. It will most likely develop into a discussion about stereotypes and their inaccuracies (see also Challenging stereotypes, pages 62).

Teaching ideas

◆ Revise sports and hobbies. Brainstorm.

◆ Discuss similarities and differences in everyday life between France and the United Kingdom.

◆ Pupils could mime activities and say what they are doing in French. Alternatively, you could play a game of *Jacques dit* (Simon Says).

◆ Try this hot potato activity. Give each table a large sheet of paper. Each table has two minutes to write as much as they know about the lives of French and English pupils. Pass the sheets around (giving two minutes for each sheet), until each table has written on every sheet. Share and discuss findings.

◆ If possible, invite a native speaker/French Learning Assistant in to talk about their hobbies as a child.

◆ Pupils could write a postcard home from France detailing the activities they have done, in French.

Vocabulaire	
mes passe-temps	my hobbies
je joue …	I play …
du piano	the piano
du violon	the violin
de la flûte	the flute
de la guitare	the guitar
je joue au …	I play …
foot	football
basket	basketball
rugby	rugby
volley	volleyball
hockey	hockey
golf	golf
je joue à la playstation	I play on my playstation
je joue à l'ordinateur	I play computer games
je fais du vélo	I cycle
je fais de la gymnastique	I do gymnastics
je fais du judo	I do judo
je fais de l'athlétisme	I do athletics
je fais du karaté	I do karate
je fais de l'équitation	I go horse riding
je fais de la voile	I go sailing

Comparing pastimes

16

Nom: Date:

Write a letter or email in French to your French friend about your hobbies.

Write a list of questions in French you would ask a French person about their hobbies and pastimes.

And now for some RESEARCH!

Use authentic resources – Internet, magazines and newspapers – to investigate how children in other countries spend their free time. In groups present your findings to the rest of the class.

Quick quiz

◆ Brainstorm some hobbies in French.
◆ How do you give opinions in French?

Halloween
Halloween

Background information

Halloween began in the British Isles as a festival called Samhain. It was believed that on this day spirits rose from the dead. So people wore masks to scare bad spirits away. Centuries later, in the 1840s, Halloween found its way to America with the Irish immigrants. Over time, it developed into the festival that we now know.

Halloween is not a traditional French holiday. But the French began to hear about it from tourists, and in their English lessons.

In 1996, the village of St. Germain-en-Laye held a Halloween party on 24th October in the middle of the day, to give locals an idea of what it was all about. Children dressed up and wore masks and pumpkins were carved and lit.

In France, children now dress up in scary costumes for Halloween. People have parties or go out for a meal. Trick-or-treating is also becoming more common. At first, children went to shops and collected marzipan-filled croissants from bakeries. Now, they go from house to house and collect sweets.

Pumpkins are popular. People carve a scary face and put a candle inside. There is even a pumpkin farm on the outskirts of Paris where people can go and pick their own pumpkins. Not everyone in France celebrates Halloween as they see it as an American festival. Some, especially elder members of society, prefer to celebrate *La Toussaint* (see below).

La Toussaint
All Saints' Day

Background information

On 1st November the French celebrate *La Toussaint* (All Saints' Day). This Catholic festival is a bank holiday in France. On this day many people in France attend religious ceremonies, remember people who have died and visit cemeteries. It is customary to leave wreaths made out of chrysanthemums on the graves. The French never give chrysanthemums as a gift because they are so closely associated with *La Toussaint* and death.

French Festivals and Traditions KS3
© *Nicolette Hannam, Michelle Williams and Brilliant Publications*

Teaching ideas

◆ Use flashcards to teach the pupils Halloween-related vocabulary. Pupils could then use cards made from page 61 to play Pelmanism (Pairs) or snap to reinforce the vocabulary.

◆ Anagrams – you could muddle up the letters of the words for pupils to unscramble.

◆ Design a Halloween poster in French, and include some spooky French words.

◆ Make *La tarte d'Halloween* (pumpkin pie) using the recipe on page 60.

Vocabulaire

un fantôme	a ghost
un crâne	a skull
un déguisement	a costume
un vampire	a vampire
une maison hantée	a haunted house
une sorcière	a witch
des bonbons	sweets
un squelette	a skeleton
une araignée	a spider
un mort vivant	a zombie
une citrouille	a pumpkin

La tarte d'Halloween

Ingredients
300 g pumpkin
4 apples
3 egg yolks
50 g sugar
75 g butter
pastry

Instructions
◆ Use a rolling pin to roll out the pastry.

◆ Put the rolled pastry into the dish.

◆ Prick the pastry with a fork.

◆ Carve out the pumpkin.

◆ Peel the apples.

◆ Cut the apples and the pumpkin into small pieces and put them in a saucepan.

◆ Cook until they are soft.

◆ Add the butter.

◆ Add the egg yolks and the sugar.

◆ Mix.

◆ Put the mix in the pastry, in the dish.

◆ Bake for 20 minutes.

◆ Bon appétit!

Ingrédients
300 g de citrouille
4 pommes
3 jaunes d'œufs
50 g de sucre
75 g de beurre
De la pâte à tarte

Instructions
◆ *Étalez la pâte avec le rouleau à pâtisserie.*

◆ *Disposez la pâte à tarte dans le moule.*

◆ *Piquez la pâte avec une fourchette.*

◆ *Creusez la citrouille.*

◆ *Épluchez les pommes.*

◆ *Coupez les pommes et la citrouille en petits morceaux et mettez le tout dans une casserole.*

◆ *Faites cuire pour obtenir une compote.*

◆ *Ajoutez le beurre.*

◆ *Ajoutez les jaunes d'œufs et le sucre.*

◆ *Mélangez.*

◆ *Versez le mélange sur la pâte, dans le moule.*

◆ *Faites cuire au four pendant 20 minutes.*

◆ *Bon appétit!*

French Festivals and Traditions KS3
© Nicolette Hannam, Michelle Williams and Brilliant Publications

Halloween words

un fantôme		une sorcière	
un crâne		des bonbons	
un déguisement		un squelette	
un vampire		une araignée	
une maison hantée		un mort vivant	

Challenging stereotypes

Background information

Everyone has visual images in their heads of places they have never been to and people they have never met. Even after visiting a country, a full picture may not have been acquired. Stereotypical expectations of French people are that they wear berets and carry baguettes around! Perhaps a little exaggerated! Stereotypical images of British people are that they always carry umbrellas, drink tea and speak with posh accents. Stereotypes can be identified for many countries and cultures, and are often very inaccurate.

Stereotypes need to be addressed, discussed, challenged and corrected. It is a subject that can be discussed as part of many lessons, or even after playground fallouts. After discussion, pupils will conclude that French pupils are very similar to themselves, with some distinct cultural differences that should be explored and celebrated.

Teaching ideas

◆ Class discussion: What is a stereotype? Can you think of any examples?

◆ Brainstorm other types of stereotypes that exist. Are they positive or negative? Discuss.

Challenging stereotypes

17

Nom: Date:

Write a letter or email in French to your French friend asking them about themselves.

Write a list of questions in French you would ask a French person about their way of life.

And now for some RESEARCH!

Use authentic resources – Internet, magazines and newspapers – to investigate how children in other countries live their lives. What do they eat/wear/do? In groups present your findings to the rest of the class.

Quick quiz

◆ What is a stereotype?
◆ How do you think people from other countries perceive British people?
◆ What stereotypes are associated with British people?

Role models

Background information

All children need good role models. Although different in each culture, common themes will remain. Pupils should be encouraged to look up to authors, sports people and so on. This will help them to become ambitious. It can provide them with real-life reasons to perform and achieve well at school.

Examples of good role models in Britain are David Beckham and J K Rowling. In France, pupils admire Thierry Henry and Vanessa Paradis.

Full name: Vanessa Chantal Paradis
Date of birth: 22 December 1972
Place of birth: Saint-Maur-des-Fossés, Val-de-Marne, France
Height: 1.60 m

Vanessa Paradis is one of the most beautiful French actresses. She was a model and a singer before she became a film-star. Her first success was the song 'Joe Le Taxi', which was a success in 15 countries. 'Joe Le Taxi' spent 11 weeks at the top of the French chart.

She has since appeared in several films, most famously Noce Blanche, for which she won the 1990 César Award for Most Promising Actress; La fille sur le pont (also known as Girl on the Bridge) in 1999 and Mon Ange in 2004

Her partner is Johnny Depp and they have two children. Her idols as a child were James Dean and Marilyn Monroe.

Full name: Thierry Daniel Henry
Date of birth: 17 August 1977
Place of birth   Les Ulis, Essonne, France
Height   1.88 m

Thierry Henry plays as a striker for the French national team and FC Barcelona, a Spanish club.

He was born and brought up in the tough neighbourhood of Les Ulis, Essonne (a suburb of Paris) where he played for an array of local sides as a youngster and showed great promise as a goal-scorer. He was spotted by AS Monaco in 1990 and was signed instantly. He joined Arsenal in 1999 and was Arsenal's top goal-scorer for almost every season he played for the club. In June 2007, after eight years with Arsenal, he transferred to FC Barcelona.

Henry has enjoyed similar success with the French national squad. Off the pitch, as a result of his own experience, Henry is an active spokesperson against racism in football.

Teaching ideas

◆ Talk about what makes a good role model.

◆ Pupils could discuss their role models. Who? Why?

◆ Pupils could draw a picture of their role model and write reasons around it.

◆ Pupils could compare a French role model to a British one.

◆ Pupils could write an acrostic poem using 'Role model' or the name of their chosen role model.

◆ Prepare a multimedia presentation about a famous French person. Create a mock interview.

Cuisine française

French food

Background information

Food is an important part of French culture. The French spend a long time preparing food and usually sit down as a family to eat. Breakfast (*le petit déjeuner*) is a quick meal before work or school, perhaps some jam and bread, or a croissant. Drinks would include hot chocolate, coffee or fruit juice. Some people dunk their croissant in their hot chocolate or coffee.

Lunch (*le déjeuner*) is a school meal for pupils on weekdays as they do not take packed lunches. There would normally be three courses (see pages 51–55 for more information). After school most children have a snack (*un goûter*) of, perhaps, jam and bread as the evening meal is quite late.

All the family would sit down for dinner (*le dîner*) later in the evening, 7.00–8.00 pm. There would be several courses and the meal would not be rushed. A typical menu would be a simple starter, followed by a meat or fish dish, then cheese, and finally dessert or fruit. There would be plenty of bread and a jug of water. Adults would most probably have wine.

Bread is a very important part of the French diet. People may buy bread daily from a *boulangerie* (bakery), or perhaps from *le supermarché* (the supermarket). Most people eat traditional baguettes (French sticks), usually sliced and without butter. Cheese is also a very important part of the diet with many types from the different regions of France.

Each region of France has a speciality and some dishes have become national, or even international, favourites. Brittany is famous for seafood (*les fruits de mer*) and for pancakes (*les crêpes*). *Fondue*, a delicious mixture of cheese and white wine that you dip bread into, originated in the Alps. More fruit and vegetables are used in the south due to the warmer climate, therefore ratatouille is popular. Some dishes, such as *coq au vin* and *foie gras*, are popular throughout France.

In addition to shops, every French village and town will also have *la Mairie* (the Town Hall) (as each has a mayor), *l'église* (the church) and *une place* – a town or village square with a *café* or *bar*.

Teaching ideas

◆ Pupils could revise the names of the shops that food comes from, eg *du pain* (bread) from *la boulangerie* (the bakery). List as many shops and food items for each as you can.

◆ Compare shops in France to those in Britain. In both countries many people now shop in large supermarkets to save time.

◆ Use the Internet to compare other buildings and places in a town. Discuss.

◆ Link to maths. Pupils could use co-ordinates to direct each other around a French town to do their shopping (See *Vocabulaire* box for vocabulary.)

◆ Pupils could design and make a board game based on places in a French town centre.

◆ Pupils could role play buying items in a shop, first as a whole class and then in small groups or pairs. They could extend their learning by adding size or colour information.

◆ Role play being in a café.

◆ List your school dinner (or packed lunch) today in French.

◆ Make a *quiche* using the recipe on page 67.

◆ Can you plan some activities for French pupils to do in school to teach them about Britain? Who could they learn about? What music could they listen to? Which places should they find on a map?

Vocabulaire

le petit déjeuner	breakfast
le déjeuner	dinner
le dîner	evening meal
le goûter	snack
le vin	wine
la baguette	French stick
le fromage	cheese
la boulangerie	bakery
la pâtisserie	cake shop
la charcuterie	butcher's
le marché	market
le supermarché	supermarket
les magasins	shops
Allez tout droit	Straight on
Arrêtez-vous	Stop
Allez-y	Go
Tournez à gauche	Turn left
Tournez à droite	Turn right
Retournez	Go back

French Festivals and Traditions KS3
© Nicolette Hannam, Michelle Williams and Brilliant Publications

Quiche

Quiche is a baked dish consisting of eggs and milk in a pie crust. Quiche Lorraine, named after the Lorraine Region in France, has bacon added to the egg mixture. However, you can include many things such as cheese, vegetables, meat and spices. Let your pupils choose what to include in their gourmet recipe!

Ingredients
1 frozen pie crust
3 eggs
1 cup milk
Other optional ingredients: grated cheese *(just enough to cover the bottom of the dish)*, meat, vegetables, spices

Instructions
◆ Preheat the oven to 375°F / 190°C.

◆ Bake the pie crust for 10 minutes.

◆ Beat together the eggs and milk.

◆ Add the cheese *(if you are using it, as the first layer on top of the pie crust)*.

◆ Add chopped vegetables or meat.

◆ Add eggs *(until the pie crust is full)*.

◆ Bake for 40–45 minutes *(or until firm)*.

◆ Bon appetit!

Ingrédients
1 pâte surgelée
3 œufs
1 tasse de lait
Choisissez d'autres ingrédients: le fromage râpé, la viande, les légumes, les épices

Instructions
◆ *Préchauffez le four à 375°F / 190°C.*

◆ *Faites cuire la pâte pendant 10 minutes.*

◆ *Battez les œufs et le lait.*

◆ *Ajoutez le fromage.*

◆ *Ajoutez la viande ou les légumes.*

◆ *Ajoutez les œufs.*

◆ *Faites cuire pendant 40–45 minutes.*

◆ *Bon appétit!*

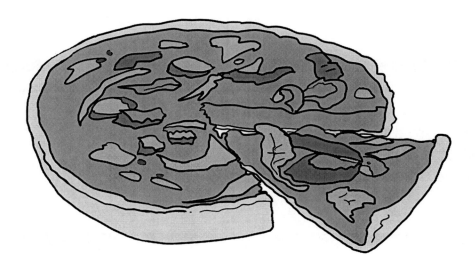

Cuisine française

Pupil Task Sheet

18

Nom: Date:

Write a letter or email in French to your French friend about your favourite food and drinks.

Create a mock interview in French surrounding food and drink and preferences.

And now for some RESEARCH!

In groups, investigate a region in France and list key information about the food and produce in this area. Present your findings to the rest of the class.

Quick quiz

- ◆ What are the mealtimes called in France?
- ◆ What is *le goûter*?
- ◆ Name some typical French foods – in French.

French Festivals and Traditions KS3
© Nicolette Hannam, Michelle Williams and Brilliant Publications

What I know about France

Nom: Date:

I can think about what I already know and what I would like to find out about France.

What do you already know about France?

What would you like to find out?

How can you find out this information?

What could you tell a French person about your country and your culture?

Extension activity

What activities could French children do in school to help them learn about Britain?

Beaujolais nouveau wine tradition

Background

French wine is produced in several regions throughout France, as shown on the map. Some of the best-known regions are Champagne, Bordeaux, Alsace, Bourgogne and Beaujolais. French wine plays a very important economic role as one of France's major exports.

The production of French wine has its origins in 6th Century BC in Marseille. The monks carried on the tradition in the Middle Ages, tending the vineyards and these wines were seen as superior.

The Loire Valley is famous for its many châteaux and vineyards.

Beaujolais nouveau is a red wine made from Gamay grapes produced in the Beaujolais region of France. It is officially released for sale on the third Thursday of November.

Beaujolais has always made a wine to celebrate the end of the harvest and selling wine within weeks of the harvest became a great way to make money. This idea soon spread across France and indeed across Europe and to the USA. 'Beaujolais Day', or 'Beaujolais Nouveau Day' is heavily promoted by its producers and has become famous worldwide, as has the slogan '*Le Beaujolais nouveau est arrivé*' – or 'The new Beaujolais has arrived.'

Teaching ideas

◆ Look out for signs and posters promoting 'Beaujolais nouveau' in November.

◆ Design your own wine label using the name of your school, for example, 'Château Battyeford'.

◆ Use the Internet to find out more about the origins of wine making.

◆ Search on the Internet for some information on French castles or *châteaux*.

Vocabulaire	
le vin rouge	red wine
le vin blanc	white wine
une bouteille	a bottle
une étiquette	a label
les raisins	grapes
le vignoble	a vineyard
un château	a castle

Joyeux Noël
Happy Christmas

Background information

Christmas is a very important religious festival in France. Many people go to church during the festive period. The way it is celebrated varies slightly in each region. In Northern France the tree (*le sapin*) is not decorated until Christmas Eve. In the Alps, a shepherd brings sheep into the church during Midnight Mass.

La fête de Saint-Nicolas – 6th December

La fête de Saint-Nicolas is celebrated mostly in northern and eastern France, as well as in Germany, Belgium, Holland and Luxembourg. Many towns have carnival processions where Saint-Nicolas arrives and throws sweets to children. Children hang up a stocking, or put shoes outside their bedroom doors, and receive sweets each morning if they have been good. This lasts until the 25th December. Parents may also give their children small gifts on the 6th December.

La veille de Noël – 24th December

On la veille de Noël many families attend Midnight Mass. Traditionally Christmas Eve dinner (*le réveillon*) was eaten afterwards and adults exchanged presents. However, these days many families eat *le réveillon* prior to Mass (but wait till afterwards to give presents). Children open their presents when they wake up on Christmas Day. A traditional Christmas meal usually consists of oysters, foie gras, stuffed turkey or goose and chocolate log (*la bûche de Noël*).

Christmas Day – 25th December

Christmas Day is spent quietly as a family. The children unwrap their presents. There is no Boxing Day in France so everyone returns to work on the 26th December.

La Saint-Sylvestre (New Year's Eve) – 31st December

In France there are lots of parties and fireworks to see in the New Year, perhaps with some French champagne. In Paris, people can choose to go to the Moulin Rouge for a cabaret show. Couples may choose a romantic cruise along the Seine.

During the festive season the Eiffel Tower is lit up and flashes on the hour every hour. On New Year's Eve there is a count down and French people see the Eiffel Tower on the television like we see Big Ben.

In Viella, in the Pyrénées, there is an annual New Year Grape Picking Contest, involving midnight mass and a torchlight procession to some mulled wine in the vineyards.

Many people combine New Year in France with skiing holidays. It is a time of celebration and great hope for the year ahead. French people often spend New Year with friends, after spending Christmas with their family.

Christmas/bonne année cards

The French tend to send *bonne année* cards to bring in the New Year, rather than Christmas cards. People only send *bonne année* cards to people who live far away and don't give them to all their friends and work colleagues. Note: when writing *bonne année* on cards, capital letters are used: *Bonne Année*.

Teaching ideas

◆ Pupils could brainstorm and label Christmas vocabulary and write a key vocabulary list.

◆ Pupils could make French Christmas word quizzes and word searches for their friends to solve.

◆ Pupils could write a simple account of the Christmas story and label a nativity scene in French.

◆ Pupils could draw and label in French some presents they would like to receive. They could also draw and label some presents they would like to give to family members.

◆ Pupils could research and label a traditional French Christmas dinner in French.

◆ Listen to some traditional Christmas carols, in both languages and compare. Use page 73 as support.

◆ Make French *bonne année* cards.

Vocabulaire

la bûche de Noël	chocolate log
Joyeux Noël	Merry Christmas
le père Noël	Father Christmas
le sapin	Christmas tree
le réveillon	Christmas Eve celebrations

un âne

Jésus

une vache

la crèche

Marie

Joseph

un mouton

un cheval

un berger

French Festivals and Traditions KS3
© *Nicolette Hannam, Michelle Williams and Brilliant Publications*

Christmas carols

Here are two popular Christmas carols. The literal translations don't make too much sense, but are useful for comparison. Comparison of the French and English words and their meanings could lead into a discussion about Christmas celebrations in different countries.

Douce Nuit
Douce nuit, sainte nuit!
Dans les cieux L'astre luit.
Le mystère annoncé s'accomplit.
Cet enfant sur la paille endormi,
C'est l'amour infini,
C'est l'amour infini!

Silent Night
Sweet night, holy night!
In the heavens, the star shines.
The foretold mystery comes true.
This child asleep on the hay,
Is infinite love,
Is infinite love!

Vive le Vent
Vive le vent
Vive le vent
Vive le vent d'hiver
Qui s'en va, sifflant, soufflant
Dans les grands sapins verts.
Oh!
Vive le temps
Vive le temps
Vive le temps d'hiver
Boule de neige, et jour de l'an
Et bonne année grand-mère!

Jingle Bells
Live the wind
Live the wind
Live the winter wind
Which goes whistling and blowing
Through the big, green Christmas trees.
Oh!
Live the weather
Live the weather
Live the winter weather
Snow balls and New Year's Day
And Happy New Year Grandma!

French Festivals and Traditions KS3
© *Nicolette Hannam, Michelle Williams and Brilliant Publications*

Joyeux Noël

19

Nom: Date:

Write a letter in French to 'Père Noël'.

Write a letter or email to your French friend about how you celebrate Christmas.

And now for some RESEARCH!

Research about Christmas in other countries using the Internet, film clips, sound files and photos. List the key information in French. Present this information to the class and evaluate each other's work.

Quick quiz

◆ How do you say 'Happy Christmas' in French?
◆ What happens on the 6th December?
◆ How is Christmas celebrated in France?
◆ What happens on New Year's Eve?

French Festivals and Traditions KS3
© Nicolette Hannam, Michelle Williams and Brilliant Publications

Planning a French Day for your school

A French Day can help to raise the profile of Modern Foreign Languages and give staff and pupils the chance to enjoy the language as a large group. You can celebrate previous successes and enthuse pupils about future learning. To give the day a bigger impact, staff and pupils can be asked to wear blue, white and red – the colours of the French flag.

When organizing the day, we recommend you provide teachers with all the resources they will need, to help alleviate stress and to allow them to participate fully in the day and enjoy themselves. On the following pages you will find lesson plans and photocopiable resources for the following four tried and tested activities:

Activity A – Henri Rousseau
Learning about the French artist, Henri Rousseau, and working as a class to make a jungle collage.

Activity B – French food
Food tasting and making a place mat.

Activity C – PE games and a song to learn
PE games/marching/dancing with instructions in French.
Learn a song and some actions for everyone to perform together in the final assembly.

Activity D – Classroom activity
Playing board games using French language.

We recommend having two assemblies: one in the morning to explain what will happen and set the tone for the day, and one at the end, so that you can celebrate your achievements. Here is a possible timetable:

Class	Session 1		Session 2		Session 3	Session 4	
1	Classroom activity	Registration	PE games then song	Playtime	Art	Food tasting	Assembly – sing the song learned during day and share work/ideas
2	Classroom activity		Song, then PE games		Food tasting	Art	
3	Art		Food tasting		PE games then song	Classroom activity	
4	Food tasting		Art	Dinnertime	Song, then PE games	Classroom activity	
5	Art		Food tasting		Classroom activity	PE games then song	
6	Food tasting		Art		Classroom activity	Song then PE games	
7	PE games then song		Classroom activity		Food tasting	Art	
8	Song then PE games	Assembly – sing some songs pupils have already learned. Explanation of day's activities	Classroom activity		Art	Food tasting	

The pupil evaluation sheet on pages 86–87 can be used to reinforce intercultural understanding and will help you to develop ideas further.

Activity A - Henri Rousseau

Objectives
◆ To learn about Henri Rousseau
◆ To make a class collage

Background information
◆ Henri Rousseau was born in 1844 in the Loire Valley in France.
◆ He moved to Paris in 1868 after his father died.
◆ He got married and had nine children. Unfortunately seven died young from tuberculosis.
◆ He started painting seriously in his 40s, and retired when he was 49 to work on art.
◆ He was self-taught and had no formal art training.
◆ His most famous paintings are of jungle scenes.
◆ Rousseau never left France so these paintings were painted from his imagination, some books and some visits to the Botanical Gardens.
◆ He painted in layers, starting with the sky in the background and ending with people or animals in the foreground.
◆ He died in 1910 in Paris.

Resources provided by MFL Coordinator
• Example of Henri Rousseau's painting 'The Equatorial Jungle'
• Large sheet of green paper for background
• Range of other coloured paper
• Laminated sheets of jungle leaves and jungle animals, one for each table (pages 77–78)
• Selection of pastels

Class teacher will need to provide
• Scissors and glue

Teaching ideas
◆ Look at Henri Rousseau's painting 'The Equatorial Jungle' (this can be found on the Internet) and explain that it depicts the jungle and is built up of lots of layers. It starts with a background and lots of tropical plants are added. Some animals are hidden in amongst the plants.

◆ You can then practise building your own jungle scene by visiting: http://www.nga.gov/kids/zone/jungle/index.htm.

◆ Pupils then have one laminated sheet of jungle leaves and one of jungle animals per table as support. They can all work on producing items to add to the class background. They can sketch them first and then cut them out. You may want to ask one group to make/draw some larger objects directly onto the background. Add objects together at the end to create a class collage.

Jungle leaf ideas

Jungle animal ideas

French Festivals and Traditions KS3
© Nicolette Hannam, Michelle Williams and Brilliant Publications

Activity B – French food

Objectives

- ◆ To taste some French food
- ◆ To know how to ask for the food in French
- ◆ To know the French names of some fruit and vegetables
- ◆ To make a place mat

Teaching ideas

- ◆ Prepare some French food for the pupils to taste. Encourage them to ask for it in French and give opinions.

- ◆ Before tasting the food teach the names of fruit and vegetables in French. There is a useful PowerPoint presentation on www.primaryresources.co.uk in Languages, Other Resources for French, Food and Drink, PowerPoint by Chris Coates.

- ◆ Give some opinions to use when tasting different foods.

- ◆ Then provide each pupil with a place mat frame to decorate during the lesson, together with laminated copies of the sheets of fruits and vegetables (one per table). The place mats can later be laminated and sent home.

- ◆ Whilst the pupils work, take around the food for them to try. Play some Paris Café music, if you have a CD, to help to pretend that you really are in France!

- ◆ Develop a cafè role-play based on the food you have provided.

Resources provided by MFL Coordinator

- • PowerPoint presentation
- • French food and drink (eg baguettes, French cheese, croissants, brioches, orange juice and hot chocolate)
- • Cups, plates
- • Laminated sheets of fruit and vegetables and their names in French, one per table (pages 80–81)
- • Place mat frames (page 82)
- • Paris café music CD and CD player
- • Laminating pouches for completed place mats

Class teacher will need to provide

- • Colouring pencils
- • Pencils/pens

Les fruits

une pomme

une poire

des fraises

un melon

des cerises

une pêche

un pamplemousse

une banane

un ananas

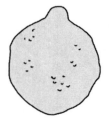

un citron

une orange

du raisin

French Festivals and Traditions KS3
© Nicolette Hannam, Michelle Williams and Brilliant Publications

Les légumes

un oignon

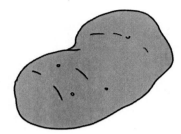

une pomme de terre

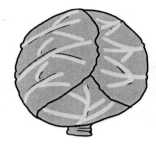

un chou

des champignons

des petits pois

une carotte

un concombre

un poivron

du brocoli

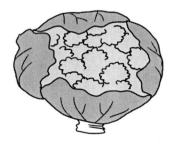

un chou-fleur

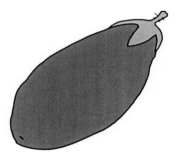

une aubergine

du maïs

Je n'aime pas :(

J'aime :)

Activity C – PE games and a song to learn

Objectives

◆ To participate in some French-themed PE games
◆ To learn a song and some actions to sing with everyone in the assembly at the end of the day

Resources provided by MFL Coordinator
• A laminated copy of this sheet
• CD and song sheet for chosen song – there are many French song books with CDs to choose from. Two recommendations are: 'Bonjour, ça va? from *Chantez Plus Fort* and 'Les sports' from *J'aime Chanter*
• CD player

Teaching ideas

◆ There are two activities to complete this session. Each class needs time in the hall or the playground to try some PE games. Start with teaching the pupils simple instructions in French:

À gauche	Left
À droite	Right
Marchez	Walk
Arrêtez-vous	Stop
Plus vite	Faster
Plus lentement	Slower
Levez	Lift
Baissez	Lower

◆ Then teach the following game. Call out instructions in French.

Les Nombres (numbers)

Give each pupil a number from 1–10. When you call out a number, those pupils run round to find a new place. Gradually use higher numbers.

◆ Back in class pupils can listen to a song and learn the words. It is even more fun if everyone learns the same actions as well. The song can be performed as a very large group in assembly.

Activity D – Classroom activity

Objective

◆ To use French vocabulary when playing co-operatively

Teaching ideas

◆ This activity consists of a selection of games the pupils can choose to play in pairs or small groups.

◆ Give each pair or group a laminated card of vocabulary to help them use some French.

Resources provided by MFL Coordinator

• Suggested games: Snakes and Ladders, Ludo, Snap or Dominoes. There are many resources available as Images on the Internet that can be colour printed and laminated (for example, Snakes and Ladders boards)
• Laminated cards to support vocabulary (page 85)

Class teacher will need to provide

• Colouring pencils
• Scissors
• Dice
• Counters

© Nicolette Hannam, Michelle Williams and Brilliant Publications

How to play games in French

◆ Choose a game to play with a friend or in a small group.

◆ Try to use some French language. Here are some useful phrases:

Tu veux jouer?	Would you like to play?
A ton tour.	Your turn.
A mon tour.	My turn.
Tu gagnes.	You win.
Je gagne.	I win.

◆ Say the number on the dice aloud.

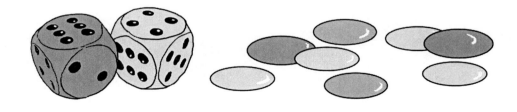

French Day

Nom: Date:

I have participated in our French Day.

In the box below, describe and evaluate the activities that took place.

French Festivals and Traditions KS3
© Nicolette Hannam, Michelle Williams and Brilliant Publications

Which activities did you enjoy? Explain why.

What did you learn?

Ask a friend what they enjoyed most and why.

Which activities would you plan for French pupils whose school was having an English day?

Useful resources
Resources available from Brilliant Publications

Chantez Plus Fort
Introduce and reinforce French vocabulary through these specially written songs. Topics include: greetings, numbers, classroom instructions, rhymes and sounds, and weather.

French Speaking Activities KS3
Activities encourage pupils to practise speaking autonomously in French. They include surveys, role-plays, presentations, quizzies, making sentences and games.

Unforgettable French
People often shy away from teaching French grammar as they feel it will be boring and involve lots of memorization. But when the focus is on looking at what things have in common, then telling or making up stories to help you remember, the learning becomes fun and the ideas stick in the brain.

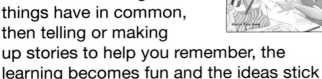

This handy book is packed full of memory tricks to help your pupils (and you!) to learn and remember key grammatical points. The attractive, fully photocopiable sheets can be handed out to pupils, made into mini-posters, or just used as memory-aides

Bon Appetit!
Follow Audrey, a Parisienne teenager, through her day and find out what French people like to eat, how and where they shop, and the importance of food in French culture.

Use the English version if your focus is on French culture, or the French version to practise French. Choose to view with or without French subtitles.

French Pen Pals KS3
Team-up with a real French school to promote language learning. This book provides a real purpose for language learning, helping to foster positive attitudes and confidence in writing French.

Contains 'fill-in-the-gap' letters for both French and English making easy communications for both schools.

Lightning Source UK Ltd.
Milton Keynes UK
UKOW010826210312

189337UK00001B/17/P